I Wrote This for Me for You

ODES, PRAYERS, AND BLESSINGS

Ellie Scott

I Wrote This for Me for You

ODES, PRAYERS, AND BLESSINGS

Ellie Scott

Aachen Publishing
St. Louis, Missouri

If I think too much about who this is for
I will forget that I owe no one anything.
No one but myself.

Also to your younger self:
May you meet them,
May you love them,
May you be so proud of them.

Foreword

The inspiration for this book, the reason I took up writing again, came from a long talk in front of a fire. The talk was with myself and to myself. I knew I'd reached an important point in my life, the crossroads where everyone says you'll make or break your destiny. I had been holding on to a relationship that was eating away the lining of my stomach (thankfully only metaphorically, at least most of the time). I felt shipwrecked: lost, damaged, and hopeless.

One day I'll be ready to write about that relationship in detail, but not yet. It hasn't been enough time for me to truly gain the perspective I need to laugh about how insane and important it was, and, in many ways, still is. What I did know is that sitting in front of that fire was my chance to cleanse my soul, to purge my system of all toxins, to shoo the monkeys from my temple. I cried, I wailed, I gnashed my teeth. At the end, I felt a different kind of emptiness. Most days, I felt hollowed out, like something was missing inside of me, leaving behind an insatiable hunger. After my dark night of the soul, I felt like a vessel. I was empty of things that no longer served me. That rotten stuffing had been removed. I was ready to be filled with things of substance: unconditional love, earth-shattering laughter, safety in the arms of a friend.

In my empty state, I wrote a letter to that relationship. I wasn't sure what would come out as I wrote by the fire, barely able to see the lines on the page through my tears. The only thing I knew for certain was that anything I had to say I needed to get out right then and there.

Below I've attached an excerpt from that letter. I wrote it with the intention of sending it to that person, but I never did. At the time, I thought I was a coward. Then I softened my heart to myself and admitted I wasn't ready to say those things our loud just yet. Now, nearly four years later, I know I only needed to see those words on the page to validate my own perspective, pain, and perseverance. I don't know if or when I'll be ready to share that story with you, so please don't be angry that I've given you a mystery and a cliffhanger. It's the kind of story you tell once in a big way, or you never tell it at all. And if you've met me, you know I only do things with my whole ass.

Thank you. That's the first thing I want to say to you. Thank you for giving me the safe space to be myself and grow and learn and figure out what it takes to be the best version of myself. So many beautiful memories with you that I'll cherish forever. But now I want to say goodbye.

I didn't know I needed you to be angry with me more. Or to criticize me. Or tell me I was wrong. I could do no wrong in your eyes. You let me believe that whatever I was doing was the right thing. It was the best decision. It was the smartest decision. It would turn out right no matter what. You believed in me so much I started trying to sabotage things and fail so you would see how imperfect I am. How dare you not speak my imperfections. How dare you not tell me I was wrong when I was. How dare you not tell me I was being irrational. How dare you let me think that I was someone I wasn't. And the key thing to remember here is that I wasn't that person. But I am her now.

What I know I want is to be loved and to give love without worry. I've been pushing people away because I knew that at some point they will know my secret. It will creep up my arm and make camp on my shoulder, taunting them to mock and jeer and run from me. But what I know is that I have a beautiful heart. I am genuine and kind and giving and loving to a point that it pains me to not do those things. And I do it without asking. Without necessity. Without question. I give love and then let that person decide if they want more. What I need and deserve is to not live in fear that this beautiful transgression we made together will be the undoing of relationships that haven't even happened yet. Relationships that are cut at the knees before they get the chance to grow and thrive. How can I fully immerse myself in any connection without the shame of my choices upon my head and on the tip of my tongue? I have to say goodbye, not just to you, but to the part of me that lives this way.

This limiting belief is holding me back from achieving my wildest dreams. It's holding me back from daring to even dream them. How could I hold myself back so much? This new world, this new phase of my life is going to be so painful and so beautiful I won't be able to comprehend it. The same way my breath would catch in my throat when I thought about our love and your smile and your body and the way we move together, our bodies and hearts and souls moving as one. That is the feeling I get when I think about where my life is headed. I will have that feeling again with the person who will transcend my concept of love and appreciation and value. He will exceed expectations I didn't know it was possible to possess or con-ceptualize. The life path I will take will be full of the most beautiful expe-riences I could only dare to dream of dreaming about. I will see the world and hear the stories that turn people into the people I know and love. I will move through the world as an observer but as a collector of stories that heal my spirit. I need to heal and to do that, I need to hear. I need to collect. I need to see. The silence comes from not speaking of our hurts. But to heal we have to speak it out. However, we do it, we have to speak out.

You have to go. And I have to let you. Our story was beautiful and it was real. And it was full of deceit and pain. There were lies we told others that we can never take back, lies we told each other that will never receive apologies, yet it is for the lies we told ourselves which we must ultimately atone. I will never look at myself again and say that I am unworthy for any reason. Even if the data proves otherwise, whatever I want I shall have. I shall be abundant. I shall be creatively fulfilled. I shall be loved beyond measure. I shall give of myself whenever and however I am able. I shall receive with an open heart and a grateful countenance.

Whatever I felt about myself and my place in this world is gone. It has disappeared and cannot surface because it has been banished from my spirit. I am healed and cleansed. I am born anew as the version of me who shares and gives and loves and receives the beauty and bounty of this world without question. I say "thank you" and "more blessings, please" and that is all.

Here I am, standing at a precipice I never thought I would see. At the place and time and moment where I let go of who I was and fully embrace the person and world of my dreams. I'm going to fuck things up. I'm going to make the wrong move. I'll say the wrong thing, and it will all be ok. No worlds will cease to exist. Nothing will fall apart that cannot or should not be repaired. I am embracing who I am and who I was and who I will be. I love her, every version of her more than the last. And now I am leaving you behind.

Tomorrow's sunrise will bring the peace and joy and perfection I seek. And if I don't find it that sunrise, it will come with another. Or the one after that. The important thing is that I will never stop giving up on the promise of sunrise.

I love you. Truly, I do. And I love me more.

That said, I am incredibly grateful your eyes will grace these pages. It is a scary and strange thing, to write a book that is your heart in print for all the world to see. I feel both liberated and terrified at the same time.

Great gobs of gratitude to the people who have touched this project in some way. No word of encouragement or help with formatting or kind review has gone unnoticed and appreciated. The word for immense gratitude of this kind does not exist, and if it does I don't know it. If it's out there, it still cannot possibly encapsulate how deeply humbled I am that you have my soul in your hands.

With greatest love,
    Ellie Scott

August 16, 2022

I wrote this for me for you

I wrote a letter once
One you'll never read,
One I'll never send.
I tore myself open
To write words for you
Then I realized
I wrote them for me.

Antipode

If I burrowed into my soul
To seek the other side
What treasures would
Await me there?
Surely there can only be
Beauty on the other side
Because where I am now
Feels anything but.

Plant my head in the ground
My toes in the air
Would I find the soil
Easier to breathe?
The air is thick with pain
Choked with sorrow
Unbreathable yet vital.

The firmness of earth
Under my feet and hands
As I crawl through the dirt
Searching for the light
The pinprick of a beam
To guide me to the surface
Gasping and grateful
For oxygen and solace.

What if I dig too far
Falling through my molten soul
Into a different atmosphere
That releases its grip
On my drifting body.
Will I live with the stars?
Will they recognize themselves in me?
Will my humanity
Banish me back to earth?

I want to know myself
Through the eyes of the opposite
See grace where I feel undesired
Feel joy where shame resides.
The soul in my chest
Deserves careful inspection
Not to find flaws or spots to improve
But to be fully understood
And in understanding, loved.

Overthinking

I thought
Then rethought
Then I thought again
This time deeper
And longer
Nails dug right in
Sunk into our mouths
Until words become flesh
Flayed open
Left broken
Wounds bare on our chest.
Then you thought
That I thought
That you thought not at all
About pain and misjudgment
Never would call
Oh my heart
Now it flutters
With love and withdrawal
For your thought
And my thought
Weren't the same after all.

Vilified

Neglected.
Unprotected.
Not being believed.

Chin up'd.
Shut up.
Unable to grieve.

Silenced.
Violenced.
Pressed to the wall.

Rushed.
Crushed.
Must run, can't crawl.

Autumnal

Leaves on the ground around my feet
Wind whips round and through my bones
Takes my breath and chills the stones
That line this quiet empty street.
Those sunny days no longer greet
Me as walking, quiet and alone,
I think on how I shall atone
For sins committed when life was sweet.

My heart believes the death of warmth
Will cleanse my soul of shame and grief
But I know my heart's true wish:
To be content as is, at peace.

When winter's chill ceases to be
May spring bring forth new life for me.

Spell

One for well wishes
One for prayers spoke
One for my darling,
My blessing, my hope.

One for long friendship
One for deep love
One for my sweetheart,
My star from above.

One for more patience
One for less fear
One for my dearest
My precious, my dear.

One for soft kisses
One for big dreams
One for my treasure
In my eyes, you gleam.

One for your heart
One for mine too
One for long days together
May we forever be true.

Valse de la Lune

I used to believe
A full moon begat
An empty sky.
Upon completion
The slate wiped clean.
Start afresh
The cycle renewed
We begin again.

The moon is rarely noticed
Unless she is full,
When she is her most complete,
Her most spectacular.
We also remark when
She is absent,
Our world darkened,
The night sky emptied.

When she fades into nothing
Or gestates toward fullness
We think little of her,
Pay no heed to her journey,
Notice the beauty of our sky
But not the progression
Of phases moment to moment
From antiquity to eternity.

It's the waxed and waned
We remember least.
Only the newness and completion
Worthy of note.
Yet they are just two moments
Significant, distinct,
Two steps in a waltz
Across the heavens above.

We Are Here

Leave your cares at the door
Shed the mask you wear
Come home to my heart
Here we are, we are here.

Quiet your mind with me
Drop the armor to the floor
Rest your head on my chest
You are here, I am too.

Slow your heartbeat down for me
Let your body melt into the bed
Take my hand and bring me down
We are one, you and me.

soft.

Hold me.
Yes, I am strong.
Just hold me.

Caress me.
Yes, I am sharp.
Caress me anyway.

Protect me.
Yes, I am brave.
Protect my bravery.

Praise me.
Yes, I am divine.
Offer praise at my feet.

Nourish me.
Yes, I am self sufficient.
Revive me with your nourishment.

Love me.
Yes, I am love defined.
Fill my world with your love.

Idolatry

When I look for my body
In the pages and screens of life
I only find her in places
Where a statement must be made.
Where someone else can point
And say, "bodies can look like this.
We can tolerate this body.
This body is acceptable."

Then I found my curves in a museum
Lavishly painted centuries ago
By masters of art
Surrounded by flowers and silks
Holding hands with other women
Fleshy and plump,
Stomachs round and soft.
"Here", the artist says, "is a woman,
A woman I know whose body
I celebrate." We say,
"If he sees her beauty
Maybe we should, too."

It wasn't until I traveled back
Millennia into the past
Beyond art for pleasure
Beyond art for fame
To the time of art for worship
To the deities of early women
Found deep in the soil by nervous hands
That I saw myself as divine
Revered as a goddess
My appeasement paramount.

My round hips mean longevity
Strong thighs mean survival.
Soft stomachs can withstand blows
And create the future,
Replicated in form and thought.
The smallness of my breasts
Gives easy access to my heart
My arms large to hold
The bounty of harvest,
To make space for the loveless.

My body is too divine to be
Worshiped by modern eyes.
My curves are prehistoric
To be held in devoted careful hands
Revered for my significance,
My vitality and substance.
Necessary as weapons that protect
Salves that heal
Knowledge of the heavens
Am I, the goddess of humanity.

Duality

Show me a woman
Who stands in her truth
And I'll show you a girl
Who lived life in a corner.

Show me a woman
Who gives selflessly of herself
And I'll show you a girl
Who had to earn love.

Show me a woman
Who strives for greatness
And I'll show you a girl
Who had to prove her worth.

Show me a woman
Who lifts up her sisters
And I'll show you a girl
Who was cast aside.

Show me a woman
Who loves her body today
And I'll show you a girl
Who was taught to fear its magic.

Show me a woman
Who has pride in herself
And I'll show you a girl
Who fought to become her.

There is such beauty in duality.

Solitude

Sleeping on one side
Of my bed
Reminds me that
The other
Won't always be
Empty.

Villain

If you want to know how a villain is born,
Ask them how often they chose their own verbs.

Kintsugi

Bring every tool
Bring gold leaf
To plaster my cracks
When I am whole again.

verbs

Fill me.
Feel me.
Fulfill me.

Pull me.
Peel me.
Prepare me.

Grate me.
Grind me.
Gratify me.

Absorb me.
Adore me.
Absolve me.

Open me.
Hope in me.
Only me.

knowledge

Teach me how loved and worthy I am
I want to know what worth looks like to you
What love means through your eyes.

Guide me through forgiveness and trust
I want to know how you hurt
So when it happens I am able to heal.

Create me within your imagination
I want to know how I measure up
But never see the rubric for your standard.

Capture me with translucent bonds
I want to know the walls of your affection
How I am kept and free and at peace with both.

Take me apart piece by part
I want to see how you come to understand me
The way you fit me together to fit together.

if/how

If you've never seen the sun
Rising after a night on the brink,
How can I describe the feeling
Of relief, of release, of renewal?

If you've never felt your heart
Implode at the sight of love
Felt for another, no longer for you
Loss has long passed your door.

If you can smell the scent of home
Wrapped around and within you
You'll never understand what it's like
To be in a desert of longing.

If your skin doesn't shrink and crawl
When you remember your shame
The sound of a world shaken loose
Will be foreign; be grateful.

Tools

With every honest conversation with my head about my heart
I wield a sledgehammer to knock down the monuments we built to
collective hurts.

When I say "no more" to actions that wound and words that scald,
I swing a battle axe to split the world of suffering from that of joy.

Each time I let go when the weight is too much, I pry up a floorboard in
the foundation of our brokenness.

We can break chains.
We can mend fences.
We can reveal.
We can rebuild.

dissolve

Every moment I hold on to pain
Never meant for me to bear
is a moment I sit
writhing in a pit
filled with venom,
with vipers,
disease-ridden air.

For each second I spend
reliving trauma and hurt
is a second I steal
from a life full of zeal
denied freedom
no options
no chance now to heal.

You are gone from this place
Yet I stay frozen stiff
No breath in my lungs
like you've cut out my tongue
"share nothing"
"tell no one"
no songs to be sung.

The pit has a bottom
The healing begins
My song will return
Self-dissolving will end.

spoken into existence

I have a love that holds but does not bind
One that carries but does not contain.
A place for healing but not to be fixed
Sanctuary but not solitary.

I have a love that fills but does not fill
One that covers but does not stifle.
A home for my heart without a fixed address
Connected to your heart but not tied.

I have a love that is true but is not truth
One that defines but does not determine.
A gift we build together as surprises for ourselves
Brand new yet broken in.

I have a love that is used but not for use
One that grows but does not outgrow
A tensile thing both tender and triumphant
Battle-tested but not hardened.

I have a love that is secure but is free
One that is work but does not need it
A gentle reminder that needs no resetting
Rested in, rested upon, and rested assured.

Thawing

You were here.
I could feel you
Sense the flash of your light
Before the crash of your thunder
The heat of your flame
Melting the ice of my heart,
A glacial relic since you left.

Then Go

If given the chance
You would leave me behind
Not a slight backward glance
Nor a note left to find.

Should opportunity arise
You'd desert me again
Leave my watering eyes
Spilling into my hand.

When the option appears
You know you won't stay
Confirm all my fears
By you leaving this way.

Certainty

Of the things I need most from love
Doubt is what I need least from love.

When standing beside you with others close
I need never to question or mistrust your love.

If my hand covers yours in a moment of hope
You'll have mine forever along with my love.

Would you come back to me, arms outstretched
Give me time for my heart to remember our love?

Poured out from my chest and left in an urn
Mourning loss and rejection, the memory of love.

Extra

My parents got a healthy child
After one lost too soon.
They also got a baby boy
Their hearts flew to the moon.
But in between they got a spare
An extra, unexpected
Not the boy or baby one
Left all alone, rejected.

Confession

I gave my heart to you
But I never shared the news
I let you think it was still mine
To give to whom I choose.
You asked if I could think of ways
To find my soul's true mate
When all the time my heart was thine
Pretending it was fate.
Can you forgive me now you know
Could we make up lost time?
Or has the time for love flown past
Our hearts' great wish denied?

Hymn

The song in my heart
Is mostly discordant notes
Trapped in a melody of
Sharps and flats.
Irregular time, unexpected crescendos
But your constant love adds
A predictable beat
Weaves beauty into the chaos
Slows the tempo
Gives my pulse a new rhythm.

Zenith

The purity of moonlight
Will cleanse my soul
Lay bare what ails me
Reveal where I lack.
The sun's strong rays
Will warm my heart
Burn away what is shallow
Give life where growth begins.
The time between each zenith
Leaves me wondering
How life can be so full
Yet also barren.

Names

Writing letters in your specific sequence is
Like asking my fingers to pour acid on themselves.
Yet I know that the healing will come from
The searing of my rotten, festering, pustuled flesh.

sprint

I've been running for so long
It feels good to sit down
With Grief, Shame and Rejection
Just to hear each one out.

bravery

I am an acrobat
in the big top
with no partner
no safety net
throwing myself out
above the crowd,
trusting in my own ability
to both catch myself
and break my own fall.

Lava

Take your time and melt me down
Find the ore at my center
Make me molten again.

Savor

Suffocate me with all that is you
Let your essence heighten my senses
Make the adrenaline in my veins choose
To drown in all that is you.

Consume all of me
Overindulge.
There will always be more.

Devastated

I live for the moments in my day
Where I am reminded of you
When my soul is briefly crushed
And I am happier for it.

The Marianas Trench

At the deepest depth of my despair,
I sink
to the
ocean
floor.

Not the blue waters of vacation shots
but the
empty
inky
pit.

My brain cannot fathom the journey below
is there
air there?
do I
care?

The pressure compresses, my will dissolves
there's no
fight left
here, I've
tried.

Nothing survives this far down in the sea
sightless
creatures
void of
thought.

The warmth in my veins leaves my body to freeze
resigned
to let
it all go.

Then the star of my universe lights up the dark
you reach
me where
none else
could.

Thank You

You know who you are and
what you did and I love you for it.

About the Author

Ellie Scott is a creative soul, storyteller, mentor, poet, and passionate word-smith who has spent her life filling the cups of others. As a shining beacon in her community, Ellie has always been the person to whom the hurt and the weary go to for help. She founded the Gogetterism movement to help inspire people to commit to pursuing their own happiness, cast off the expectations of others, and build a world of compassion and solidarity. She currently resides in Saint Louis, Missouri, where she enjoys listening to her dog Charlemagne snore and finding the best burger in town.

For more information about Ellie,
or to become a Go-getter yourself,
visit her website at www.elidansco.com.

CPSIA information can be obtained
at www.ICGtesting.com
Printed in the USA
JSHW040112150922
30466JS00007B/205